Gratitude

Unlocking God's blessings and benefits

**Archbishop Nicholas
Duncan-Williams**

Gratitude
Unlocking God's blessings and benefits

ISBN: 978-1-948233-04-0
Copyright ©2019 Nicolas Duncan-Williams
All rights reserved solely by the author. The author guarantees all contents are original and do not infringe upon the legal rights of any other person or work. No part of this book may be reproduced, shared in a retrieval system, or transmitted in any form or by any means, electronic, mechanical, photocopying, and recording, without prior written permission of the Author/Publisher.

For further inquiries and for training materials, please contact the publisher.

Published in 2019 by:
GOSHEN PUBLISHERS LLC
P.O. Box 1562
Stephens City, Virginia, USA
www.GoshenPublishers.com

Cover Design by:
GOSHEN PUBLISHERS LLC

10 9 8 7 6 5 4 3 2

A profitable life is founded upon a thankful heart, whose posture acknowledges God and the divine helpers He has sent for the fulfillment of purpose and destiny.

TABLE OF CONTENTS

Introduction i
Chapter 1: What is Gratitude?..1
Chapter 2: Remember where You Began with God 11
    How did Israel Forget 13
    The Children of Israel Forgot God 17
    A Reminder of Gratitude to Israel 22
Chapter 3: Gratitude, Not Murmuring.. 25
    Praise in Place of Murmuring!... 35
    Don't Murmur like Gideon 37
    David Demonstrates Gratitude 40
    Dancing before the Ark 40
    Paul Teaches against Murmuring 42
Chapter 4: Watch that Blessing 47
    The Blessing 48
    Remembrance Formula:.. 50
    The Case of Lucifer 54
    Every Good Gift is from God 58
Chapter 5: Don't Forget your Friends 61
    God Believes in Friendship... 62
    Acknowledge the People God Uses 64
    Joseph in Egypt 65
    Create a Book of Remembrance... 71
Chapter 6: Acknowledge your Father(s)....................................... 73
    Learn from Elijah and Elisha 79
    Avoid being an Absalom 83
    Bless what Blessed You.. 84
Chapter 7: Simply be Thankful 87
    Learn from Hannah... 90
    Let us Learn from the Lepers Jesus Healed 93
    Making Thanksgiving a Lifestyle 97
Chapter 8: Benefits of Gratitude 99
    Gratitude and Multiplication 100
        The Miracle of the Five Loaves and Two Fish................. 100
    Gratitude is the Key to Longevity 103
    Gratitude brings Wholeness.. 104
    Gratitude brings Promotion 105
    Gratitude when you Face New Challenges............................. 106
    Gratitude in Prayer & Worship 107
    Gratitude while Facing the Impossible 108
Conclusion 111

INTRODUCTION

I was prompted to write this book about gratitude because, having served for more than four decades in ministry, I recognize it as God's way to lasting success. I have come to realize that gratitude plays a major role in determining the outcomes of many life choices and the fulfillment of destiny. Nevertheless, many people fail to see its strategic significance, and why it must be practiced, taught, and established in the very core of our being.

In my travels around the world, I have seen many people, families, organizations, churches, and even nations lose their way and their blessings, all due to their lack of understanding of gratitude. Because of ingratitude to God, they have plunged into all manner of chaos, crises, and major problems. "The wicked shall be turned into hell, and all the nations that forget God" (Psa 9:17).

Some of the major denominations, churches, and ministries, are deeply divided and have endangered the legacy of faith that was once delivered to them by the saints. They have forsaken the ancient landmarks and that has resulted in challenges of magnitudes that we have never witnessed. Organizations and businesses are crumbling, including those that the world thought were too big to fail. Leaders across the world are grappling with fear and don't know what to do.

In addition to all this, we have a generational problem looming. There is a new generation that does not understand the importance of gratitude. The Apostle Paul warned us that this problem of ingratitude would be one of the major signs of the end times.

"This know also, that in the last days perilous times shall come. ² For men shall be lovers of their own selves, covetous, boasters, proud, blasphemers, disobedient to parents, unthankful, unholy, ³ Without natural affection, trucebreakers, false accusers, incontinent, fierce, despisers of those that are good, ⁴ Traitors, heady, highminded, lovers of pleasures more than lovers of God; ⁵ Having a form of godliness, but denying the power thereof: from such turn away." (2 Tim 3: 1-5)

God, in His redemptive wisdom, is burdening me as a father to teach, train, guide, and impart wisdom through this material into this generation and those to come. It is my prayer and my hope that the principles in this book will minister to you, create a major shift, and equip you to make quantum leaps in your relationship with God and with all those around you.

Journey with me through the pages of this book to access Kingdom keys that unlock the secrets of gratitude, and the benefits and rewards it has in store for us!

CHAPTER 1: WHAT IS GRATITUDE?

*"Gratitude is not only the greatest of the virtues
but the parent of all others."*
                                        Marcus Tullius Cicero

Gratitude as defined by the Merriam Webster Dictionary is, "The State of being grateful", or "thankfulness". It is described in the Oxford Dictionary as, "the quality of being thankful; readiness to show appreciation for and to return kindness". Gratitude, I believe, is an attitude, a mindset, a posture of the heart, an aroma, a fragrance, and a disposition that always reveals who we are to the core.

Gratitude determines our altitude. It was the key that revealed the secret behind King David's elevation. It is this same key that provides the methodology that can take one from the lowest to the highest places in life, from nobody to somebody. David went from a poor shepherd boy to becoming one of the greatest kings that ever lived.

Gratitude, as a Kingdom culture, must be rooted in love, and understanding of grace and God's goodness. In business, gratitude is reflected in our investment in customer service.

Gratitude in the life of a very blessed person is always evidenced by how they give back. Saying, "thank you", is so powerful and amazing when it is done well and especially when the setting is right. It motivates. It encourages. It is a booster. It makes people who help you recognize that you care. It shows that you are grateful for their time, sacrifices, thoughtfulness, efforts, support, and investments in you. This changes outcomes and does great wonders in business, relationships, ministry, marriage, families, and even amongst nations.

From a biblical and spiritual standpoint, gratitude is the natural response that God expects from all His children. It is **an attitude and a culture** that He wants embedded in us. He wants it reflected in everything we say and do. Simply put, gratitude must be our attitude on a consistent basis in order to enjoy all the blessings God bestows upon us.

This attitude of gratitude eventually determines our altitude in God and in life. Likewise, it affects how we stand in the midst of challenges and adversity. Gratitude was the reason for the institution of the different feasts and celebrations for the children of Israel. The Lord ordained them as part of their worship to deliver them from idolatry and ingratitude. He wanted them free from the seduction of worshipping the blessing instead of the blesser, or the creation instead of the Creator.

The common mistake found in humanity is the tendency to forget. Hence, God divinely established celebrations in the spirit of thanksgiving, so that man does not forget. God instituted, for example, the Passover as a symbol of Israel's deliverance from Egypt (Exo 12). It also serves as a pointer of God's redemptive plan for the entire human race through the sending of His

Son to die as the Lamb of God for all mankind. Jesus echoed the words of the Father, when He said to his disciples, "as often as you do this, do this in remembrance of me" (1 Cor 11:25). The essence of this was to create a culture of gratitude. It was meant to be passed on from generation to generation so as to guarantee continuous cycles of blessings and favor from God.

As a father in the Kingdom, I see the need to teach generations the importance of developing the attitude of gratitude. All should be taught to say, "thank you", for not just the big things, but also the little things that God has done for us. A habit of appreciating one another and learning to celebrate those who have been a blessing to us along the way, is a major Kingdom key.

Reflecting on my life and ministry, I am eternally grateful for the pivotal role that the late Archbishop Benson Idahosa, of blessed memory, played in my life and at the inception of my ministry, as a father. His example is still helping me in my spiritual growth and development. And for that, I am eternally grateful.

> **The virtue of gratitude is an innate human expectation. When anyone takes time to do something nice or good for someone else, they usually anticipate an expression of appreciation.**

For example, when someone opens a door for you, compliments you, gives you an opportunity or a nice gift, the natural response should be to say, "thank you". This is among our principle ethics and core values as Kingdom citizens. It must be interwoven into the fabric of all of our interactions.

Celebration, and not just tolerance, is the atmosphere that activates the power of gratitude. It builds lasting friendships and divine partnerships that help us fulfill the desires of God's heartbeat without frustration and delay. When nations' foundations are rooted in God's grace and mercy they will practice this principle of gratitude. The result will be a positive global impact. However, those who ignore this important life principle unfortunately enter into a difficult path of captivity, struggles, frustration, and eventually irreverance.

To the great leaders of our world, endeavor to always practice and master the art of thanksgiving to God. Always show gratitude to your citizens and all those who are your helpers and burden bearers of your goals and objectives. If you do this, it shall be well with you, your posterity, your nation, and your legacy forever.

So, why should we show God gratitude? Well, the main reason is that in ourselves we can do nothing. The life we have, the opportunities we get, the grace to will, the wisdom and the strength to do, all come from Him. It is only He who offers grace, opportunity, favor, life, and the power to get wealth (Deu 8:18).

In the words of A.W. Tozer, "Gratitude is an offering precious in the sight of God, and it is one that the poorest of us can make and be not poorer but richer for having made it."

When we see gratitude as an offering, it changes our perspective. For example, trying to find a gift for a powerful person who seems to have everything is very difficult. Gratitude then becomes a precious gift only you can give. God cannot give Himself gratitude, only you can.

Furthermore, we can always give this gift regardless how rich or poor we are, which makes a big difference. We must see it as a necessity, which is not based on performance or what we think He has done or hasn't done. Your gratefulness to Him should be based on His goodness and all that Christ sacrificed for you. This frame of mind gives our gratitude a strong and solid foundation, which is not easily shaken by trials, temporary challenges, or what we may be going through. This is what the Bible calls the sacrifice of thanksgiving, where our gratitude is like offering a sacrifice of continual praise, no matter what (Heb 13:15).

David said, "I will bless the Lord at all times: His praise shall continually be in my mouth" (Psa 34:1). All times includes the good times, bad times, difficult times, and challenging times. Nevertheless, His praise, gratitude, thanksgiving, and appreciation will always be in my mouth!

My hope is that this book will minister to you as it is ministering to me. I believe that the revelation of gratitude will unlock and accelerate a greater dimension of success, greatness, and the fulfillment of destiny in your life. I believe wholeheartedly that it is one of the major keys to guarantee the flow of God's continual blessings in your life.

It is my prayer that the Body of Christ will become unified in continuously growing a heart and a lifestyle of gratitude that always says, "Thank You, Lord!"

Additionally, I pray that we tremendously bless all those we've come across who by design are, or were, channels of blessings in our lives.

Chapter 2: Remember where You Began with God

*"Ingratitude is a crime more despicable than revenge,
which is only returning evil for evil,
while ingratitude returns evil for good."*

William George Jordan

If there is one consistent thing I have done in all of my years of ministry, it is to share my testimony of what the Lord has done for me as well as where I began with God. This simple, but amazing, act of remembrance has been key to the many successes in my life and ministry, and has encouraged millions around the world impacting their faith by causing them to believe that if He did it for me, He can also do it for them.

The act of remembrance, and not being ashamed, has been one of the greatest expressions of my gratitude to God. It is also a constant reminder that softens my heart toward people, gives me a passion for souls, makes me humble myself before Him, and keeps me grateful.

I am also thankful that the Father gives us an opportunity to learn from the mistakes of others. For instance, the children of Israel had successes, but they also made some serious mistakes. One major mistake they made was not giving thanks to Elohim for all the mighty miracles He did for them. They were so blinded and distracted by the problems before them that they forgot everything; but how could Israel forget?

How did Israel Forget

To appreciate what God did for Israel, we must look at their condition prior to God's deliverance from Egypt.

"Therefore they did set taskmasters over them to afflict them with their heavy burdens. They built for Pharaoh store cities, Pithom and Raamses. But the more they were oppressed, the more they multiplied and the more they spread abroad. And the Egyptians were in dread of the people of Israel. So they ruthlessly made the people of Israel work as slaves and made their lives bitter with hard service, in mortar and brick, and in all

kinds of work in the field. In all their work they ruthlessly made them work as slaves." (Exo 1:11-14)

"Then the Lord said, "I have surely seen the affliction of my people who are in Egypt and have heard their cry because of their taskmasters. I know their sufferings, and I have come down to deliver them out of the hand of the Egyptians and to bring them up out of that land to a good and broad land, a land flowing with milk and honey, to the place of the Canaanites, the Hittites, the Amorites, the Perizzites, the Hivites, and the Jebusites." (Exo 3:7-8)

"The same day Pharaoh commanded the taskmasters of the people and their foremen, "You shall no longer give the people straw to make bricks, as in the past; let them go and gather straw for themselves. But the number of bricks that they made in the past you shall impose

on them, you shall by no means reduce it, for they are idle. Therefore they cry, 'Let us go and offer sacrifice to our God.' Let heavier work be laid on the men that they may labor at it and pay no regard to lying words." (Exo 5-6:9)

From the passages above, we see that the children of Israel were in a state of despair, hopeless, and it looked as though they would be slaves in Egypt forever. However, their Heavenly Father turned things around in accordance with the promise He made to Abraham more than 400 years earlier.

"Then the Lord said to him, "Know for certain that for four hundred years your descendants will be strangers in a country not their own and that they will be enslaved and mistreated there. But I will punish the nation they serve as slaves, and afterward they will come out with great possessions." (Gen 15:13-14)

This was fulfilled when God called Moses and empowered him to go and set His people free. What a mighty God we serve! He had a plan for them even before they went into bondage and, in the fullness of time, He brought them out as a mighty nation. Seventy of them went into Egypt, but it is believed over 3 million came out.

Revisiting this story makes me want to encourage you to pause for a moment and walk down memory lane and reflect on what your life would have become if Jesus had not given you an invitation to change your life. I believe that if the Children of Israel had only taken time to meditate on what the Lord had done for them, their hearts would have been submerged in such a sweeping wave of joy, gladness, and thankfulness.

Just like Israel, humanity on innumerable occasions has been victim to slavery and bondage on so many levels. They do not only present themselves physically but spiritually, mentally, psychologically, financially, socially, relationally, etc. But why did this happen to Israel?

THE CHILDREN OF ISRAEL FORGOT GOD

"Both we and our fathers have sinned; we have committed iniquity; we have done wickedness. Our fathers, when they were in Egypt, did not consider your wondrous works; they did not remember the abundance of your steadfast love, but rebelled by the sea, at the Red Sea. Yet he saved them for his name's sake, that he might make known his mighty power. He rebuked the Red Sea, and it became dry, and he led them through the deep as through a desert. So he saved them from the hand of the foe and redeemed them from the power of the enemy. And the waters covered their adversaries; not one of them was left. Then they believed his words; they sang his praise. But they soon forgot his works; they

did not wait for his counsel. But they had a wanton craving in the wilderness and put God to the test in the desert; he gave them what they asked, but sent a wasting disease among them". (Psa 106:7-15)

Here are ten reasons why Israel forgot God. These are also lessons to help us avoid repeating the same common mistakes:

1. Israel had a sin and iniquity problem.
2. Their hearts were wicked.
3. They did not consider the way God works.
4. They did not remember the abundance of his steadfast love.
5. They were rebels, disloyal to God and Moses.
6. They were quick to forget the goodness of God and did not show gratitude.
7. Whenever they faced problems and insurmountable odds, they did not seek God's counsel.
8. They were carnal with lustful desires and kept testing God. They even spoke death to themselves, which eventually happened.

9. They stopped keeping the statues of God and disconnected themselves from His blessings.

10. After being in captivity and bondage for more than 10 generations, they lost faith in God and they just wanted to go back to Egypt.

We are also not immune to these mistakes. In every person there is a proclivity to forget God as a result of ingratitude. Take heed to these warning signs.

This passage is an acknowledgement King David made well after Israel had settled in the Promised Land. Although blessed and favored, David was a man of reflection and knew the importance of engaging God. He understood that leaders who take responsibility instead of shifting blame in times of weakness and vulnerability, will instinctively remember God, humble themselves before Him, and not forget to show gratitude.

David masterfully took the mistakes of his forefathers and used it as a blueprint to rise above their mistakes. He chose to remember the God who put fear in the nations that Israel encountered when they were simply a crowd wandering in the wilderness, marching toward their land of promise. David chose to remember the victory of Israel over Jericho, and the crossings of the Jordan and the Red Sea. This is one of the vital acts of his life that made him different from Saul and all those that would follow after him.

David's sense of gratitude was a part of him and every opportunity he had, he always testified about where he began with God. Intense thanksgiving, praise, and passionate worship, were his lifestyle.

> "Gratitude makes sense of our past, brings peace for today, and creates a vision for tomorrow."
>
> **Melody Beattie**

Fear is one of the by-products of one's focus on self and not on God. Gratitude helps us overcome debilitating obstacles like fear. When David faced Goliath he remembered that it was God who helped him overcome a bear and a lion, so he went into battle with confidence.

"And David said unto Saul, Thy servant kept his father's sheep, and there came a lion, and a bear, and took a lamb out of the flock: And I went out after him, and smote him, and delivered it out of his mouth: and when he arose against me, I caught him by his beard, and smote him, and slew him. Thy servant slew both the lion and the bear: and this uncircumcised Philistine shall be as one of them, seeing he hath defied the armies of the living God. David said moreover, The LORD that delivered me out of the paw of the lion, and out of the paw of the bear, he will deliver me out of the hand of this Philistine."

(1 Sam 17:34-37)

The more grateful you are to God the greater the chance of seeing more of His intervention. A grateful person recognizes God in the little things and positions them for greater blessings or breakthroughs.

A Reminder of Gratitude to Israel

Before they entered the Promised Land, God gave the children of Israel a graphic presentation of the land that He was bringing them into, and was very intentional in adding the reminder that they were to bless Him for the good land He had given them, and not forget His goodness.

> "For the Lord your God is bringing you into a good land, a land of brooks of water, of fountains and springs, flowing out in the valleys and hills, a land of wheat and barley, of vines and fig trees and pomegranates, a land of olive trees and honey, a land in which you will eat bread without scarcity, in which you will lack nothing, a land whose stones are iron, and out of whose hills you can dig copper. And

you shall eat and be full, and you shall bless the Lord your God for the good land he has given you."(Deu 8:7-10)

I see the Lord bringing you not just into a physical land alone, but also into a land of promises filled with many, awesome blessings beyond your wildest imagination. The key is to always remember to be grateful. Never forget to say, "thank you", for where you are now. If you remain grateful, God will bring you into so much more, and I know that it will absolutely blow your mind.

CHAPTER 3: GRATITUDE, NOT MURMURING

*"Grumbling and gratitude are,
for the child of God, in conflict.
Be grateful and you won't grumble.
Grumble and you won't be grateful."*

Reverend Billy Graham

Delay in waiting especially for something good to happen, a dream to come through, an expectation to be fulfilled or the manifestation of a promise can often bring discouragement. If not handled well, this can open the door to the spirit of murmuring, complaining, grumbling, ingratitude, and destruction.

Throughout their journey in the wilderness, one attitude that often got the Israelites in trouble with God was murmuring. Webster's Dictionary defines murmuring as "a half-suppressed or muttered complaint". In other words, trying to suppress the complaint, and yet still saying it quietly. One of the most dangerous killers of destiny is murmuring and complaining instead of using the same tongue to express gratitude.

The Israelites continuously murmured and complained about everything. They literally fought God and Moses every step of the way. God did not like it and He never hid His displeasure from their grumbling attitude. The following texts capture the numerous occasions where they complained and murmured against Moses and against God.

1. **You have made us enemies of Pharaoh**

Israelites accused Moses and Aaron saying, "ye have made our savour to be abhorred in the eyes of Pharaoh, and in the eyes of his servants, to put a sword in their hand to slay us". (Exo 5:21-22)

2. **You have brought us into the wilderness to die**

"And they said unto Moses, Because there were no graves in Egypt, hast thou taken us away to die in the wilderness? wherefore hast thou dealt thus with us, to carry us forth out of Egypt? Is not this the word that we did tell thee in Egypt, saying, Let us alone, that we may serve the Egyptians? For it had been better for us to serve the Egyptians, than that we should die in the wilderness." (Exo 14:11-12)

3. **You have brought us into the wilderness to die of thirst**

"And when they came to Marah, they could not drink of the waters of Marah, for they were bitter: therefore the name of it was called Marah. And the people murmured against Moses, saying, What shall we drink?" (Exo 15:23-24)

4. You have brought us into the wilderness to die of hunger

"And the whole congregation of the children of Israel murmured against Moses and Aaron in the wilderness: And the children of Israel said unto them, Would to God we had died by the hand of the LORD in the land of Egypt, when we sat by the flesh pots, and when we did eat bread to the full; for ye have brought us forth into this wilderness, to kill this whole assembly with hunger." (Exo 16:2-3)

5. You have brought us into the wilderness to die of thirst

"And all the congregation of the children of Israel journeyed from the wilderness of Sin, after their *journeys, according to the commandment of the LORD, and pitched in Rephidim: and there was no water for the people to drink. Wherefore the people did chide with Moses, and said, Give us water that we may drink. And Moses said unto them, Why chide ye with me? wherefore do ye tempt the LORD? And the people thirsted there for water; and the people murmured against Moses, and said, Wherefore is this that thou hast brought us up out of Egypt, to kill us and our children and our cattle with thirst?" (Exo 17:1-3)*

6. You have abandoned us
"The Israelites enter into idolatry and dance before the golden calf." (Exo 32:19-29)

7. There was no reason for the complaint
"And when the people complained, it displeased the LORD: and the LORD heard it; and his anger was kindled; and the fire of the LORD burnt among

them, and consumed them that were in the uttermost parts of the camp." (Num 11:1)

8. You have failed to uphold the laws of God by marrying a non-Israelite

"And Miriam and Aaron spake against Moses because of the Ethiopian woman whom he had married: for he had married an Ethiopian woman. And they said, Hath the LORD indeed spoken only by Moses? hath he not spoken also by us? And the LORD heard it." (Num12:1-2)

9. You have brought us into the wilderness so that we might be slaughtered

"And all the congregation lifted up their voice, and cried; and the people wept that night. And all the children of Israel murmured against Moses and against Aaron: and the whole congregation said unto them, Would God that we had died in the land of Egypt! or would God we had died in this wilderness! And wherefore hath the LORD brought *us unto this land, to fall by the sword, that our wives and our children should be a prey? were it not better for us to return into Egypt? And they said one to another, Let us make a captain, and let us return into Egypt." (Num 14:1-4)*

    10.   You have brought us into this land so the inhabitants of this land will kill us

"The Israelites desired to stone to death, Caleb and Joshua, son of Nun for giving a good report concerning taking the Promise Land and its inhabitants." (Num 14:10)

    11.   You have made yourself holier than us

Korah, Dathan, Abiram and On, established a rebellion against Moses. (Num 16)

    12.   You have murdered the people of God

"But on the morrow all the congregation of the children of Israel murmured against Moses and against Aaron, saying, Ye have killed the people of the LORD." (Num 16:41)

13. You have brought us into the wilderness to die of thirst

"And there was no water for the congregation: and they gathered themselves together against Moses and against Aaron. And the people chode with Moses, and spake, saying, Would God that we had died when our brethren died before the LORD! And why have ye brought up the congregation of the LORD into this wilderness, that we and our cattle should die there? And wherefore have ye made us to come up out of Egypt, to bring us in unto this evil place? it is no place of seed, or of figs, or of vines, or of pomegranates; neither is there any water to drink." (Num 20:2-5)

14. You have brought us into the wilderness to die of hunger and thirst

"And they journeyed from mount Hor by the way of the Red sea, to compass the land of Edom: and the soul of the people was much discouraged because of the way. And the people spake against God, and

against Moses, Wherefore have ye brought us up out of Egypt to die in the wilderness? for there is no bread, neither is there any water; and our soul loatheth this light bread." (Num 21:4-5)

The murmurings of the Israelites progressively got worse as noted in Numbers 14, when they not only spoke or murmured against Moses but they murmured against God.

The sad and serious thing about their murmuring was that they did not only complain about the situation they were going through, but they used it as an opportunity to compare their current experiences to Egypt. In other words, they preferred to be in slavery and bondage than go on a journey with God that was now beginning to look too long for them.

At that period in time there were no enemies threatening them. In fact, God had blessed them with their every need to the extent that even their clothes and shoes were growing with them. They had a pillar of cloud by day, fire by night, and God was feeding them; yet, they despised it and called it worthless. They allowed the seed of murmuring to become a part of their attitudes and behavior. This was a critical weakness in their character that caused them to continually be in trouble with God. It was as if they were always looking for any and every opportunity to complain and to prove to God and Moses that the idea to bring them out of Egypt was a mistake. It sounded like the deliverance by His mighty acts was of no use. God's response was swift and to the point as He sent fiery serpents to bite anyone who complained.

After a while some of the people figured out why they were being bitten and repented. God subsequently offered a solution by asking Moses to make a serpent made of brass. Moses was instructed to hang the serpent on a tree so that anyone bitten by the fiery serpent only had to look up, and be healed. This was a foreshadow of

God's provision for their salvation and healing, through Christ being crucified and looking unto Him by faith producing healing and life. Yet, many today prefer to reject God's provision, like Israel did by murmuring, complaining, ignoring His provision, and would rather die than to look up and live.

Praise counters murmuring and it activates and strengthens one's faith. It is a catalyst for blessing and, by design, it causes a person to remember all that God has ever done for him. When we praise, God's goodness fills our hearts and reinforces the hedge of God's protection, blocking the clandestine advances of the devil.

> **A Christian who moves in praise and not murmuring becomes a threat to the enemy and makes it extremely difficult for the devil to manipulate them.**

PRAISE IN PLACE OF MURMURING!

"Though the fig tree should not blossom, nor fruit be on the vines, the produce of the olive fail and the *fields yield no food, the flock be cut off from the fold and there be no herd in the stalls,* [18] *yet I will rejoice in the Lord; I will take joy in the God of my salvation.* [19] *God, the Lord, is my strength; he makes my feet like the deer's; he makes me tread on my high places."* (Hab 3:17-19a)

The Prophet acknowledges that challenging situations are a part of life. This scripture depicts a picture of famine, dryness, poverty, and eventually death, should nothing change. He presents that in these difficult moments one may be tempted to murmur, grumble, and complain. He exhorts us to give God praise.

The truth is that our temporary difficulty and challenging situations doesn't change God or His plans and purposes for our lives. God is still God!

Don't Murmur like Gideon

Gideon was threshing wheat in a winepress when God sent and angel to him who addressed him as a mighty man of valor. However, his immediate response to that greeting was a complaint.

"Now the angel of the Lord came and sat under the terebinth at Ophrah, which belonged to Joash the Abiezrite, while his son Gideon was beating out wheat in the winepress to hide it from the Midianites. And the angel of the Lord appeared to him and said to him, "The Lord is with you, O mighty man of valor." And Gideon said to him, "Please, my lord, if the Lord is with us, why then has all this happened to us? And where are all his wonderful deeds that our fathers recounted to us, saying, 'Did not the Lord bring us up from Egypt?' But now the Lord has forsaken us and given us into the hand of Midian." And the Lord turned to him and said,

"Go in this might of yours and save Israel from the hand of Midian; do not I send you?" And he said to him, "Please, Lord, how can I save Israel? Behold, my clan is the weakest in Manasseh, and I am the least in my father's house." (Jud 6:11-15)

Can you believe that after such a glorious and empowering greeting from an angel, the immediate words that came out of Gideon was that of grumbling and complaint? Gideon was tired of the Medianites and didn't see an end to their plundering. The promises of God were far from his mind based on his present circumstances. He had to hide the wheat in the winepress so that it was secured.

Gideon was not celebrating the fact that an angel sent by God had come to herald God's plan to use him to deliver his people from the Midianites. Seven years of hardship and delay in seeing the salvation of God made him skeptical. He wanted to see the hand of the Lord in his day.

Gideon also felt inadequate to this invading horde. He felt that God must be mistaken to think He can use him to fight this mass of people. So, he suggested that God look for someone else because he did not see himself as qualified to lead Israel. If you follow the story well, you will see what God had to do to eventually get Gideon to agree and be willing to become His instrument to eventually defeat the Midianites. If God had not been patient with Gideon, He would have destroyed him. Murmuring and grumbling seems to have taken the better part of the children of Israel despite all that they saw God do to their enemies.

You know that once again God showed His mighty power by using 300 men to defeat an army of a million. Do we really have any justifiable reason to complain when we encounter difficult situations?

> God has proven to us that His presence is always with us, even when difficult situations arise.

DAVID DEMONSTRATES GRATITUDE

King David is an example of one who lived a life of gratitude. He contrasts the people of his day and the other kings of Israel in many ways. The Psalms are full of David's appreciation to God for the many things God did for him. One of such is the popular story about David dancing before the Ark of the Covenant, and in the process, he exposed himself.

DANCING BEFORE THE ARK

"And David returned to bless his household. But Michal the daughter of Saul came out to meet David and said, "How the king of Israel honored himself today, uncovering himself today before the eyes of his servants' female servants, as one of the vulgar fellows shamelessly uncovers himself!" And David

said to Michal, "It was before the Lord, who chose me above your father and above all his house, to appoint me as prince over Israel, the people of the Lord—and I will celebrate before the Lord. I will make myself yet more contemptible than this, and I will be abased in your eyes. But by the female servants of whom you have spoken, by them I shall be held in honor." And Michal the daughter of Saul had no child to the day of her death."
(2 Sam 6:20-23)

In Michal's opinion, David was the King and had to behave himself well before men. What she was not aware of was that the presence of God and knowing the Lord meant everything to David. He was happy to have the Ark of the Covenant returning to its proper place, and in the order that God prescribed. His outward expression of joy and exuberance to God pales in comparison to the gratitude and worship He deserves!

When Michal admonished David, she activated an insurmountable weight of gratitude that was so full in his heart that it began to overflow. The deeper we entrench ourselves in gratitude, all fiery arrows of humiliation, disgrace, dishonor, embarrassment, indignity, discretization, scandal, and contempt is repelled and backfires back into the camp of our accusers. In other words, gratitude creates a shield that becomes an impenetrable fortress around our identity in Christ.

It was God who took David from the pasture to the palace and this same God was with David everywhere he went. David's journey with God caused him to cultivate a heart of gratitude and worship. He became one of the greatest worshippers and the greatest king of all time.

Paul Teaches against Murmuring

"Nor should we put Christ to the test, as some of them did and then died from snakebites. And don't

grumble as some of them did, and then were destroyed by the angel of death. These things happened to them as examples for us. They were written down to warn us who live at the end of the age. If you think you are standing strong, be careful not to fall." (1 Cor 10:9-12)

Paul teaches us on the unfortunate side effects of a heart that doesn't invest in gratitude but instead invests in murmuring. He draws attention to what happened to the children of Israel in the wilderness as a result of murmuring and complaining. Many of them died in the wilderness. This was a hefty price for God as this was his inheritance and He aspired for them to live long and experience the Promise land.

However, He has exalted His Word above His name and there is nothing He could to protect them from that fate. So, He sent Paul to show us the blueprint of what not to do, so that He may not suffer this kind of a loss again. Let's empty ourselves of any murmuring that counters the realization of God's Promise Land for us. Rise up child of God and let's sow seeds of gratitude until the world sees the manifestation of His glory in our lives.

Gratitude affords us the opportunity of giving God the glory He deserves. It brings us closer to God and builds foundations of godly obedience within us. The Scripture narrative shown here makes it very clear that God desires for us to adopt a lifestyle of gratitude in whatever situations we find ourselves. After all, the things we go through here in this life is only temporal. The greater and more prosperous and glorious life lies ahead of us after we have endured until the end.

A person with a heart full of gratitude constantly keeps the testimonies of the Lord before his eyes. God commanded the Israelites to tell the stories of His ways, His deliverances, and power unto their children and their children's children, so they would grow up to know the

Lord. If we follow this example, when trials and tribulations come, we will always have something to thank God for and to rejoice in Him.

Every day I aspire to count my blessings and name them one by one. The hymn writer reminds us that it will surprise us to see what the Lord has done for us. There is absolutely no question that identifying God's goodness is more beneficial to us than focusing on the troubles the devil deploys against us. Our God is always to be praised and thanked for being there for us. He has constantly demonstrated that He keeps promises and we are blessed and highly favored to be His children.

Repeat after me: I have purposed in my heart, that day by day, I will constantly renew my mind with the truths of gratitude, and with deep sincerity, I solemnly pledge that with the help of Elohim, my heart's conviction and posture, will be positioned, entrenched, and fortified in gratitude.

Chapter 4: Watch that Blessing

*"Thou that hast given so much to me,
Give one thing more, a grateful heart."*

George Herbert

There are so many lessons we can learn from God's relationship with the Children of Israel. One of them is the attitude of gratitude God expected from them when the promise came. Before they entered the land of promise God gave the Israelites what could be described as a "remembrance formula": a way to remember all that He had done for them.

The Blessing

God promised them houses they did not build, a multiplication of their flocks and herds, etc. He hoped that with those manifold blessings right before their eyes they would forever remember the God of their deliverance from slavery and the God of abundant provision. He expected them to look upon those things and give thanks continually for all the provision and protection He afforded them.

Here's the account of God's forewarning to them:

"Take care lest you forget the LORD your God by not keeping his commandments and his rules and his statutes, which I command you today, lest, when you have eaten and are full and have built good houses and live in them, and when your herds and flocks multiply and your silver and gold is multiplied and all that you have is multiplied, then your heart be lifted up, and you forget the LORD your God, who brought you out of the land of Egypt, out of the house of slavery, who led you through the great and terrifying wilderness, with its fiery serpents and scorpions and thirsty ground where there was no water, who brought you water out of the flinty rock, who fed you in the wilderness with manna that your fathers did not know, that he might humble you and test you, to do you good in the end. Beware lest you say in your heart, 'My power and the might of my hand have gotten me this wealth.' You shall

remember the LORD your God, for it is he who gives you power to get wealth, that he may confirm his covenant that he swore to your fathers, as it is this day. And if you forget the LORD your God and go after other Gods and serve them and worship them, I solemnly warn you today that you shall surely perish. Like the nations that the LORD makes to perish before you, so shall you perish, because you would not obey the voice of the LORD your God." (Deu 8:11-20)

REMEMBRANCE FORMULA:

Take care, lest you forget.

1. After multiplication, your heart will be lifted up. Watch out for pride.

2. Believe in God's power and might and not your own.

3. Do not forget God. Do not worship other gods.

The cycles and the pursuits of bondage are aggressive and seek to manifest in humanity. It never seeks the bound, but it seeks those in their place of dominion. Dominion is lost when the pillars of gratitude are degraded. A grateful heart is abhorrent to a taskmaster. The virtue of gratitude aligns itself with the expectations of God. In the Scripture above we learn why Israel suffered multiple relapses with bondage, all the way from Egypt to Babylon.

Without a grateful heart, the Prophet Elijah could not have operated in such power. The power God bestowed upon him was unparalleled to any prophet of Jezebel. And it was with that power Elijah was able to call down fire from heaven and slay 850 prophets of Baal and Asherah.

In today's society, it is imperative for us to tell the works of the Lord to our children and their children. When we develop this culture of remembrance in our children, we are giving them an inheritance that will stand the test of time. In a grateful society, the knowledge of God and His goodness must become our way of life so that he can captivate both younger and future generations.

> "And it came to pass after these things, that his master's wife cast her eyes upon Joseph; and she said, Lie with me. But he refused, and said unto his master's wife, Behold, my master wotteth not what is with me in the house, and he hath committed all that he hath to my hand; There is none greater in this house than I; neither hath he kept back any thing from me but thee, because thou art his wife: how then can I do this great wickedness, and sin against God? And it came to pass, as she spake to Joseph day by day, that he hearkened not unto her, to lie by her, or to be with her. And it came to pass about this time, that Joseph went into the house to do his business;

and there was none of the men of the house there within. And she caught him by his garment, saying, Lie with me: and he left his garment in her hand, and fled, and got him out." (Gen 39:7-12)

It was the act of remembrance that caused Joseph to stay true to his conviction. Even though he was a slave, he was still grateful to his master for elevating him above all his peers.

Where there is gratitude, there is the sweet fragrance of humility and an eventual lifting up ensues. However, pride is the enemy of gratitude and when humanity refuses to be thankful to God, pride always sets in. Where there is pride, there are trace elements of ego, arrogance, and self-worship, because pride never walks alone. Furthermore, the product or end result of pride is a sense of entitlement. The mode and frequency of gratitude yields elevation, however pride always yields a great and dismal fall. At the point of blessing, the full measure of gratitude is always desired.

THE CASE OF LUCIFER

Today we know him commonly as Satan or the devil. So as not to place ourselves in a similar situation as him, it helps for us to refer to him as Lucifer. This will help us to better understand what actually happened to him and learn from his awful experience. The Prophet Isaiah tells the story of how pride and rebellion entered into Lucifer's head and resulted in his expulsion from heaven. The end result is that even to this day Lucifer is here on earth continually sowing seeds of tribulations and interrupting the peace of God's people.

"How you are fallen from heaven, O Day Star, son of Dawn! How you are cut down to the ground, you who laid the nations low! You said in your heart, 'I will ascend to heaven; above the stars of God I will

set my throne on high; I will sit on the mount of assembly in the far reaches of the north; I will ascend above the heights of the clouds; I will make myself like the Most High.' But you are brought down to Sheol, to the far reaches of the pit. Those who see you will stare at you and ponder over you: 'Is this the man who made the earth tremble, who shook kingdoms, who made the world like a desert and overthrew its cities, who did not let his prisoners go home?' All the kings of the nations lie in glory, each in his own tomb; but you are cast out, away from your grave, like a loathed branch, clothed with the slain, those pierced by the sword, who go down to the stones of the pit, like a dead body trampled underfoot." (Isa 14:12-18)

From the Prophet's narration we know that Lucifer was originally an anointed cherub (angel) who occupied a very lofty position in heaven, where he became the embodiment of music. His very presence reflected the glory of God. Imagine such an incredible endowment. However, gratitude was not found in him and iniquity penetrated his heart. This is one of the most interesting mysteries theologians have not been able to explain. He was cast out of heaven because, where he was supposed to display gratitude, he led an insurrection. We cannot worship that against which we are rebelling.

Under the conviction of gratitude, we are not able to forget who made us who we are. God accommodates a heart submerged in humility and obedience but evicts a prideful heart.

Position and power have a way of bringing out the best and worst in humanity. We grow stronger in the things of God when we emulate Him and are reduced when we sideline Him from our lives. When you have a heart birthed in gratitude, you desire more of God's will than your own will. I thank God for the assignment He has placed upon your life. I challenge you to celebrate His authority and make Him your singular source. This is the key Kingdom dominion principle. Jesus declared that we shall do greater works than Him. Because He goes to the Father and through Him, He has empowered us to propagate His kingdom here on earth!

There is a value connected to every blessing and when we search it out, we open the door to gratitude and multiple promotions within our lives. Andra Day says, "I think gratitude is a big thing. It puts you in a place where you're humble."

We have so much to be grateful for. Humility is a posture we take by the grace of God and the deep work of the Holy Spirit in our hearts. We willingly allow Him to do that work in us so that we can please Him. The Bible emphatically states: "God resists the proud, but gives grace to the humble. Therefore, "humble yourselves under the mighty hand of God, that He may exalt you in due time" (Jam 4:6b).

> **Let us be wise in walking in the grace of God above all things!**

When the children of God constantly acknowledge the grace of God in their lives, we position ourselves to receive more from Him. When we don't, the channel flow of God's blessings dries up. However, a repentant and humble heart will reconnect the flow back into that place of gratitude and the blessings will flow once again.

EVERY GOOD GIFT IS FROM GOD

The Apostle James helps us understand and remember that every good gift is from God.

"Do not be deceived, my beloved brothers. Every good gift and every perfect gift is from above, coming down from the Father of lights, with whom there is no variation or shadow due to change. Of

his own will he brought us forth by the word of truth, that we should be a kind of first fruits of his creatures." (Jam 1:16-18)

'Heavenly Father, freely you have given and continue to give to us. Give us a heart like yours that concerns itself with the downtrodden and the disadvantaged. With a willing heart that is free from judgment and endowed with humility, and by your special grace, make us the blessing that satisfies and brings wholeness to the cries of your people. Amen!'

CHAPTER 5: DON'T FORGET YOUR FRIENDS

"At times our own light goes out and is rekindled by a spark from another person. Each of us has a cause to think with deep gratitude of those who have lighted the flame within us."
                                        Albert Schweitzer

God Believes in Friendship

The Merriam-Webster Dictionary defines a friend as "one attached to another by affection or esteem", or "a favored companion". The Bible celebrates good friendships and shows us that we were made to depend on each other. No one is expected to go through life all by himself. God created us in such a way that we depend on one another. We have a corporate and individual destiny and we were created to be interdependent, to compliment and to complete each other. For example, Proverbs teach that, "A friend loveth at all times, and a brother is born for adversity" (17:17); and "Iron sharpeneth iron; so a man sharpeneth the countenance of his friend" (27:17).

The Scripture, "It is not good that the man should be alone" (Gen 2:18), though it was written in the context of marriage, is not limited to marriage. It speaks of friendships, companionship, destiny, and God-appointed relationships.

When we walk alone, we may at times miss the richness of opportunities that can come as companionship and the benefits of sharing life's joys, sorrows, dreams, and hopes with a true friend. The Preacher captured this truth perfectly when he wrote the following piece:

> "Two are better than one, because they have a good reward for their toil. For if they fall, one will lift up his fellow. But woe to him who is alone when he falls and has not another to lift him up! Again, if two lie together, they keep warm, but how can one keep warm alone? And though a man might prevail against one who is alone, two will withstand him—a threefold cord is not quickly broken." (Ecc 4:9-12)

ACKNOWLEDGE THE PEOPLE GOD USES

One of the classic stories in the Bible on friendship is the relationship between David and Jonathan. Through this unique friendship the Lord saved David's life and delivered him from the wicked plans of King Saul. Even after the house of King Saul was destroyed and Jonathan died, David still remembered his dear friend Jonathan. He did not stop at remembrance, but he expressed the need to show kindness to anyone left in the house of his father, King Saul. David fulfilled this promise by honoring and adopting his son, Mephibosheth, as one of his own, setting him at his table and giving him all his father's inheritance (2 Sam 9:1-13).

Gratitude is trans generational. To those operating in a higher order of this virtue, understand the importance of the legacy to the extent that when their friends have passed on, they remember them by being there for their families, friend's, children, or grandchildren (Exo 20:6).

God's gratitude to those who serve Him is so deep that He keeps covenant to a thousand generations of those who love Him. This is evident in the friendship between Abraham and God. Though God is sovereign and can do all things by Himself, He works through individuals and loves to partner with us to bless humanity. God can use anyone and sometimes He uses people you don't even know or would never suspect.

Before we embark on the journey of remembering our friends, we must first acknowledge every person who has contributed to our lives and helped us to become the people we are today.

JOSEPH IN EGYPT

"On the third day, which was Pharaoh's birthday, he made a feast for all his servants and lifted up the

head of the chief cupbearer and the head of the chief baker among his servants. He restored the chief cupbearer to his position, and he placed the cup in Pharaoh's hand. But he hanged the chief baker, as Joseph had interpreted to them. Yet the chief cupbearer did not remember Joseph, but forgot him." (Gen 40:20-23)

The Cupbearer was wrongfully accused and imprisoned. While in prison, God revealed the meaning of the dream to His servant Joseph. Exactly as Joseph had described, the dream was fulfilled. When the Cupbearer was restored to his former position, he forgot Joseph altogether (Gen 40:23). If you follow the narrative of the story, it was later that God worked out His plans and purpose and the truth about Joseph came up, leading to his interpretation of the king's dreams and being made prime minister of Egypt.

"Then the chief cupbearer said to Pharaoh, "Today I am reminded of my shortcomings. Pharaoh was once angry with his servants, and he imprisoned me and the chief baker in the house of the captain of the guard. Each of us had a dream the same night, and each dream had a meaning of its own. Now a young Hebrew was there with us, a servant of the captain of the guard. We told him our dreams, and he interpreted them for us, giving each man the interpretation of his dream. And things turned out exactly as he interpreted them to us: I was restored to my position, and the other man was impaled. So Pharaoh sent for Joseph, and he was quickly brought from the dungeon. When he had shaved and changed his clothes, he came before Pharaoh." (Gen 41:9-14)

Even though the cupbearer had forgotten about Joseph, God created a greater opportunity to ensure that the Cupbearer fulfilled his promise, willingly or unwillingly. When you adopt gratitude as a culture, your acts of kindness will make room for you. It will cause unthinkable opportunities and possibly even cause you to stand in the presence of greatness.

From a place of reciprocity, it is therefore in our best interest when we acknowledge the people whose contributions helped us get to where we are today. When we acknowledge them and celebrate them it is equivalent to confessing gratitude to God. Shifting the focus from ourselves is the first step to acknowledging that it was not by your own strength and power and wisdom that we are what we are today.

The Scripture declares, "In every thing give thanks: for this is the will of God in Christ Jesus concerning you" (I Thes 5:18). A thankful and grateful heart is a heart full of joy.

The call of gratitude requires us to reach out, acknowledge, and honor our friends by thanking them and praying for them.

"Oil and perfume make the heart glad, and the sweetness of a friend comes from his earnest counsel. Do not forsake your friend and your father's friend, and do not go to your brother's house in the day of your calamity. Better is a neighbor who is near than a brother who is far away." (Pro 27:9-10)

The passage teaches about friendship as the person who is closest to us and contrasts it with someone we would normally call a brother by blood but is not accessible to you in many ways. The sweetness of a friend comes from his earnest counsel. There are also those for whom our contributions into their lives have been similarly beneficial to them. When we measure the effect of such mutual sharing, we realize that they were our destiny helpers and we were in turn theirs.

I thank God for every friend who has stood by me through thick and thin. I thank Him that they enabled me to navigate through the not-so-easy path. I'm thankful that path has led me to a vast array of unexpected accomplishments, by the grace of God.

It is of great comfort to have a friend who will walk with you through the ebb and flows of life where tragedies, trials, calamity, and hardship can strike when we least expect it. A faithful companion is one who will stand with you during critical moments of your life. This is priceless and a blessing worthy of giving thanks to God.

Solomon gives us some golden nuggets in the book of Proverbs concerning the constitution of a good friendship:

> "A friend loves at all times, and a brother is born for adversity." (Pro 17:17)

"Iron sharpens iron, and one man sharpens another." (Pro 27:17)

CREATE A BOOK OF REMEMBRANCE

A great way to track and remind yourself of the blessings from God and from your friends, is by having a "Book of Remembrance" to document your experiences. The Bible is also a book of remembrance.

Chapter 6: Acknowledge your Father(s)

"For though ye have ten thousand instructors in Christ, yet have ye not many fathers: for in Christ Jesus I have begotten you through the gospel." Apostle Paul, 1 Cor 4:15

The Merriam Webster Dictionary defines father as follows: "a) a male parent, source or progenitor, usually a patriarch; b) one that originates or institutes; c) one that begets.; and d) to be the founder, producer, or author of."

Fatherhood is an eternal principle that cannot be circumvented. You cannot go around it. There are many examples in the Bible to establish the fatherhood principle. Fatherhood is not limited to the biological order. In fact, there are more fathers of non-biological order than there are of biological.

Think of Moses and Joshua, Elijah and Elisha, Paul and Timothy, just to mention a few. Note that in these examples, the sons who stayed under the tutelage of their designated spiritual fathers until the fullness of their time, did great things, sometimes greater than their fathers were able to accomplish.

Fatherhood is a process involving an individual, usually a mature person, who provides out of relevant experience Godly counsel, guidance, and support, to another. A spiritual father is one who mentors a son or daughter until Christ is formed in them, helps them to discover and maximize their potential, and then releases them to fulfill their God given destiny.

The Lord placed in my heart to honor some of the fathers and seniors in the Pentecostal and Charismatic movement in the nation of Ghana. In a special service we came together and honored celebrated and blessed them for their great contributions, sacrifices, and exemplary leadership. We didn't want to miss this God ordained time and season to celebrate them. I said, "Let's do it now, Let's not wait!" Not long after that, God responded by doing some incredible things not only in my life and ministry, but in the lives of those who stood with me and supported that great vision. What we did is nothing new, as the children of Israel had adopted that practice years ago. We can trace it all the way back in the Bible and see where God gave instructions to the children of Israel concerning fathers and children.

"Hear, O Israel: The Lord our God, the Lord is one. You shall love the Lord your God with all your heart and with all your soul and with all your might. And these words that I command you today shall be on your heart. You shall teach them diligently to your children and shall talk of them when you sit in your house, and when you walk by the way, and when you lie down, and when you rise. You shall bind them as a sign on your hand, and they shall be as frontlets between your eyes. You shall write them on the doorposts of your house and on your gates." (Deu 6:4-9)

The second one goes like this:

"Train up a child in the way he should go; even when he is old he will not depart from it."(Pro 22:6)

The Apostle Paul wrote the third, giving a similar account with an illustration of an heir inheriting what rightfully belongs to him. This is what he wrote:

"I mean that the heir, as long as he is a child, is no different from a slave, though he is the owner of everything, but he is under guardians and managers until the date set by his father. In the same way we also, when we were children, were enslaved to the elementary principles of the world. But when the fullness of time had come, God sent forth his Son, born of woman, born under the law, to redeem those who were under the law, so that we might receive adoption as sons. And because you are sons, God has sent the Spirit of his Son into our hearts, crying, "Abba! Father!" So you are no longer *a slave, but a son, and if a son, then an heir through God." (Gal 4:1-6)*

As you can see, the majority of these references portray a family scenario where a father and mother are teaching their children the ways of God. The above examples are both realistic and symbolic. They are real because heads of families are obligated by the principles of God to raise their children in the fear of the Lord. At the same time, they are symbolic because it takes more than one's biological father to help him fulfill God's divine mandate over his life.

The Bible calls this discipleship, whereas, the corporate world refers to this as mentorship. However, the common denominator in both of these is that someone is intentionally grooming another to reach his predestined potential.

Learn from Elijah and Elisha

Elijah and Elisha were not biologically connected; however, their relationship is a classic blueprint for what we now know as discipleship or spiritual mentoring. You can study the full account in the book of 2 Kings.

> *"Now when the Lord was about to take Elijah up to heaven by a whirlwind, Elijah and Elisha were on their way from Gilgal. And Elijah said to Elisha, "Please stay here, for the Lord has sent me as far as Bethel." But Elisha said, "As the Lord lives, and as you yourself live, I will not leave you." So they went down to Bethel. And the sons of the prophets who were in Bethel came out to Elisha and said to him, "Do you know that today the Lord will take away your master from over you?" And he said, "Yes, I know it; keep quiet.*

Elijah said to him, "Elisha, please stay here, for the Lord has sent me to Jericho." But he said, "As the Lord lives, and as you yourself live, I will not leave you." So they came to Jericho. The sons of the prophets who were at Jericho drew near to Elisha and said to him, "Do you know that today the Lord will take away your master from over you?" And he answered, "Yes, I know it; keep quiet.

Then Elijah said to him, "Please stay here, for the Lord has sent me to the Jordan." But he said, "As the Lord lives, and as you yourself live, I will not leave you." So the two of them went on. Fifty men of the sons of the prophets also went and stood at some distance from them, as they both were standing by the Jordan. Then Elijah took his cloak and rolled it up and struck the water, and the water was parted to the one side and to the other, until the two of them could go over on dry ground." (2 Kin 2:1-8)

Elisha followed Elijah and refused to depart from him. He went everywhere with him, serving and learning from him, all the way up to the point of Elijah's departure where Elisha had the revelation and audacity to ask for the double portion.

Remembering and honoring our fathers in the faith is of paramount importance. What I've learned over time is the secret for relevance and longevity. That is why I am not ashamed to acknowledge great men of God who significantly poured into my life and blessed me: the late Archbishop Benson Idahosa; Lester Sumrall; Dr. T.L. Osborn; Dr. Oral Roberts of blessed memory; Elders from Church of Pentecost; Dr. Morris Cerullo, whom I still call "Papa"; and many others. They all helped to shape my Christian life and experience in ministry. I still hold them in high esteem because I believe strongly in the principle of fatherhood.

The reality is that there are none among us who can boast of being self-made. This idea of being self-made is an illusion that violates the spiritual principle of fatherhood. No one is self-made. We all rise upon the wings of other people who have gone ahead of us, and we should honor and celebrate their contributions. In actuality, this practice brings a greater blessing to us because it comes from a heart of gratitude.

Pause for a moment and ask yourself the following questions: Who discipled you? Where are they now, and what are they doing? What relationship do you currently have with them? Who do you owe your spiritual paternal allegiance to? Ultimately these questions help you to determine whom you owe your spiritual and paternal allegiance.

The importance of remembering our fathers is that they sacrificed so much for us to walk in the path of their footprints. Their contributions allow us to enjoy the many liberties we experience in life and in ministry. With their toil and sweat, they have paved the way for us to enjoy the success we experience and, therefore, we need to remember them and always say "thank you!"

AVOID BEING AN ABSALOM

Absalom sat near the gate and preyed on people who were offended and discontented. He sympathized with their situations and basically told them that under his leadership things would change. He sowed disloyalty among the people and drove their affections to himself and away from God's authority figure, who was his father, King David. His actions brought rebellion into Israel (2 Sam 15:1-31).

> **This spirit of Absalom is self-serving, disloyal, and destructively influential among those whose hearts are offended with leadership.**

This spirit is fueled by pride and unbridled ambition. It pushes a person to prematurely break away from the protection of his father and makes him anxious to make a name for himself. Whereas, simply remaining loyal and applying God's principles of true sonship will cause him to soar.

Keeping a continued healthy relationship with your father is one of the most crucial kingdom principles that we should be intentional and committed to fulfill. Even in the natural, once a child is weaned, and has grown they never forget their parents. Why should the children of God do differently?

BLESS WHAT BLESSED YOU

It is a natural process that when fathers have taken good care of their children, that they in turn will reap some benefits. It's an honor to bless your father and allow the principles of accountability and honor to release blessings the way God ordained it, from the fathers to the sons and daughters as revealed in Scripture.

Isaac pronounced a blessing after his son hunted to bring venison such as the father loved. It is proper for sons to use their tools, gifts, and strength to bless their fathers, and for fathers to pronounce blessings upon their sons. When Isaac ate of the venison that Jacob brought to him, he blessed him, and God also affirmed the blessing.

CHAPTER 7: SIMPLY BE THANKFUL

*"Acknowledging the good that you already have in your life
is the foundation for all abundance"*

Eckhart Tolle

More than 25 years ago, the then president of Ghana organized the first national thanksgiving service. As providence would have it, I was invited to be one of the speakers and to play an important role in the process. Many people advised that I should decline the offer. When I decided that it was not about me, people's opinions, nor even my own feelings, but instead was about fulfilling the will and intent of God, I accepted the offer. As it is common to our experience, public opinion went into overdrive with accusations of me being partisan and becoming the media's target as they helped syndicate many lies concerning my motives.

Needless to say, I remained steadfast. I was overwhelmed that as a nation we had decided to assign a specific day for simply expressing gratitude and thanking the Lord God Almighty. We were so happy for an opportunity to publicly express our gratitude as Children of God, and to thankfully acknowledge Him for His mercies toward us as a nation.

This tradition is part of our culture, and I believe it may be one of the reasons why God has spared and delivered the nation of Ghana from destruction, civil war, and all kinds of dangers. It has never been an easy experience but sometimes thanking God comes at a cost. For instance, even now as we embark on the construction of the National Cathedral of Ghana, similar attacks have risen from many places, including men and women of God; however, it's always a good thing to give thanks to the Lord.

Child of God, no matter who fights us, attacks us, insults us, let them say what they want to say because vindication is in the womb of time and if we thank Him, He will always glorify Himself. Our Heavenly Father never fails but is excellent in all His ways!

LEARN FROM HANNAH

Consider meditating on Hannah's prayer and the important lessons God has for you regarding the power of thanksgiving.

"And Hannah prayed and said, "My heart exults in the Lord; my horn is exalted in the Lord. My mouth derides my enemies, because I rejoice in your salvation. There is none holy like the Lord: for there is none besides you; there is no rock like our God. Talk no more so very proudly, let not arrogance come from your mouth; for the Lord is a God of knowledge, and by him actions are weighed. The bows of the mighty are broken, but the feeble bind on strength. Those who were full have hired themselves out for bread, but those who were hungry have ceased to hunger. The barren has borne seven, but she who has many children is forlorn. The Lord kills and brings to life; he brings

down to Sheol and raises up. The Lord makes poor and makes rich; he brings low and he exalts. He raises up the poor from the dust; he lifts the needy from the ash heap to make them sit with princes and inherit a seat of honor. For the pillars of the earth are the Lord's, and on them he has set the world." (1 Sam 1:1-8)

Elkanah had two wives: Hannah and Peninah. Of them, Peninah had children, but Hannah had none and that created a serious rivalry. We can appreciate what a woman in Hannah's position had to go through, first from her rival Peninah, and secondly from Elkanah's family. Hannah was looked upon as the person with the problem. In the eyes of her family and in the court of public opinion, barrenness was her fault. Despite that, Elkanah did all he could to assure Hannah of his love for her, but that was not enough to bring happiness into her heart. It was clear that what would make Hannah a happy woman was giving birth to a child.

Hannah's state of being was further troubled when the High Priest could not discern a burdened heart from one that was drunk with wine. She had passed the stage of despair. What she did next is absolutely mind blowing. She prayed in a manner that changed her destiny and that of Israel. In response, God Almighty gave her a son to fulfill the prophecy. She in turn gave him back to God as an offering. When God answered her prayer, the mocking from her rival, Peninah, stopped. Those who despised her would no longer call Hannah all kinds of names. A massive weight was lifted from her, and there were no more nights of sleeplessness, anguish, and heartache. In so many ways, the birth of Samuel brought redemption in Hannah's life and changed the course of a nation.

It was Hannah's prayer of thanksgiving that shifted everything, and this is what God expects from us on a daily basis. Those who have adopted Hannah's heart are like them that sing the song, "If it had not been for the Lord on my side…" This is a song from a grateful heart that has had an encounter with God.

> **When we know the faithfulness of Our Heavenly Father, we are inspired to render quality thanks to Him. A life of spontaneous gratitude expands our personal knowledge, understanding, and revelation of God.**

Let Us Learn From The Lepers Jesus Healed

"On the way to Jerusalem he was passing along between Samaria and Galilee. And as he entered a village, he was met by ten lepers, who stood at a distance and lifted up their voices, saying, "Jesus, Master, have mercy on us." When he saw them he said to them, "Go and show yourselves to the priests." And as they went they were *cleansed. Then one of them, when he saw that he was healed, turned back, praising God with a loud voice; and he fell on his face at Jesus' feet, giving him thanks. Now he was a Samaritan. Then Jesus answered, "Were not ten cleansed? Where are the nine? Was no one found to return and give praise to God except this foreigner?" And he said to him, "Rise and go your way; your faith has made you well." (Luk 17:11-19)*

Every believer should be knowledgeable of this very popular story and the truths it endows. This miracle was an especially profound one as leprosy was such a cruel condition that not only attacked their health, but also made them outcasts. Regardless of their education or pedigree, everything in their lives was stricken: their health, their ability to make a living financially, and everything connected to their identity in society was completely decimated.

In public, lepers were required by law to cry out "unclean, unclean" so people would give way as to not physically touch them. This was the experience of the ten lepers. However, their encounter with Jesus changed all that. By His grace and mercy, they were healed and were no longer outcasts. They no longer had to cry out, "unclean, unclean". As you can imagine their hearts were overjoyed by this new way of living. They could now return to their families, occupations, and become legitimate members of society.

Despite the joy of their deliverance, it was only one of them who paused to reflect, while the others did not. As is common to man, the other nine were overtaken by excitement and, as it turned out, they only left with one blessing. Carefully notice Jesus' response. He asked the one who returned where the other nine were. His expectation was that all of them would come back to acknowledge the fact that He was the One who healed them. So, Jesus made a profound statement to the one who returned. It was not only a statement, but it was an additional blessing that brought the fullness of the miracle that the others would most likely have wished they had also returned to received. Jesus said to this one, "your faith has made you whole" (Luke 17:18-19). This declaration was the second blessing that would change the life of this one in such a dynamic way. His story and the testimony would forever be that Jesus Christ of Nazareth not only healed him but also made him whole.

Good things always come to us when we enter into a time of pause and reflection. When we do this, we allow the Holy Spirit to minister to us in those sacred moments. If we can only understand that these are divine moments where we come face to face with the reality of God, who He is and His goodness towards us.

I believe that people who give thanks to God and are generally thankful to people who have been a blessing to them will live longer. With God, the more you give, the more He gives you in return. Let us pray to God for a heart of gratitude and thanksgiving so that we may connect to the overflowing channel of God's blessings.

MAKING THANKSGIVING A LIFESTYLE

"It is good to give thanks to the Lord, to sing praises to your name, O Most High; to declare your steadfast love in the morning, and your faithfulness by night, to the music of the lute and the harp, to the melody of the lyre. For you, O Lord, have made me glad by your work; at the works of your hands I sing for joy." (Psa 92:1-4)

- Continually

"Through him then let us continually offer up a sacrifice of praise to God, that is, the fruit of lips that acknowledge his name. Do not neglect to do

good and to share what you have, for such sacrifices are pleasing to God." (Heb 13:15-16)

- Privately

"When Daniel knew that the document had been signed, he went to his house where he had windows in his upper chamber open toward Jerusalem. He got down on his knees three times a day and prayed and gave thanks before his God, as he had done previously." (Dan 6:10)

- Publicly

"I will thank you in the great congregation; in the mighty throng I will praise you." (Psa 35:18)

CHAPTER 8: BENEFITS OF GRATITUDE

"Gratitude helps you to grow and expand, gratitude brings joy and laughter into your life and into the lives of all those around you."

Eileen Caddy

Gratitude has so many advantages, benefits, and rewards. After 41 years in ministry, I can attest that gratitude is a game changer with both God and man.

GRATITUDE AND MULTIPLICATION

Whenever we are grateful for little, the favor on our life multiplies. It grows and expands exponentially. When gratitude is in action, the miracle of increase, addition, and multiplication is released.

Most of the things God gives us, begins with us. It starts as a seed and the attitude of gratitude and thanksgiving is what multiplies it.

The Miracle of the Five Loaves and Two Fish

> "He answered and said unto them, Give ye them to eat. And they say unto him, Shall we go and buy two hundred pennyworth of bread, and give them to eat? He saith unto them, How many loaves have ye? go and see. And when they knew, they say, Five, and two fishes. And he commanded them to make all sit

down by companies upon the green grass. And they sat down in ranks, by hundreds, and by fifties. And when he had taken the five loaves and the two fishes, he looked up to heaven, and blessed, and brake the loaves, and gave them to his disciples to set before them; and the two fishes divided he among them all. And they did all eat, and were filled. And they took up twelve baskets full of the fragments, and of the fishes. And they that did eat of the loaves were about five thousand men. And straightway he constrained his disciples to get into the ship, and to go to the other side before unto Bethsaida, while he sent away the people."(Mar 6:37-45)

When Jesus took the five loaves He could have been frustrated and complain of how little it was like Philip did. He didn't but rather gave thanks. It was after the thanksgiving that the multiplication began, and it was enough to feed more than five thousand.

If you are thankful for what you have you will end up having more. It creates room for more. If you despise what you have you will end up losing even that which you have.

Read the parable of the talents

"Then the man who had received one bag of gold came. 'Master,' he said, 'I knew that you are a hard man, harvesting where you have not sown and gathering where you have not scattered seed. So I was afraid and went out and hid your gold in the ground. See, here is what belongs to you.' His master replied, 'You wicked, lazy servant! So you knew that I harvest where I have not sown and gather where I have not scattered seed? Well then, you should have put my money on deposit with the bankers, so that when I returned I would have *received it back with interest. 'So take the bag of gold from him and give it to the one who has ten bags. For whoever has will be given more, and they will have an abundance. Whoever does not have, even what they have will be taken from them. And throw that worthless servant outside, into the darkness, where there will be weeping and gnashing of teeth.'"(Matt 25: 24-30)*

The man with one talent buried it. It was eventually taken away from him. Do not despise the days of small beginnings (Zec 4:10). I see the Lord multiplying the little you have and making it great, mega, and bringing you into the realm of overflow as you thank Him and bless Him for what you have. In Jesus' name, Amen.

GRATITUDE IS THE KEY TO LONGEVITY

Gratitude is the key to longevity, especially when you are grateful for your parents. Honoring your parents is the one commandment with a promise. "Honor thy father and thy mother: that thy days may be long upon the land which the LORD thy God giveth thee" (Exo 20:12). As a pillar of gratitude, this is a key principle that we must practice so we can attain longevity, happiness, and contentment. Chip Conley said, "Social scientists have found that the fastest way to feel happiness is to practice gratitude".

> **Gratitude drives out the negative emotions that normally cause grief, stress, depression, and feelings that cut people off prematurely.**

GRATITUDE BRINGS WHOLENESS

From the story of the ten lepers, we see that they were all healed but one came back to say, "thank you". That individual acted wisely by expressing gratitude. It resulted in not just healing, but wholeness. Wholeness restored him as though he never had any issue at all.

Jesus said to that leper, "thy faith has made you whole". Meaning the leper took another step beyond healing. He was made whole; that is total completeness, full restoration plus restitution of whatever was lost in every area of his life, all as a result of his act of gratitude.

The power to resolve every other need in his life was revealed to him because he gave thanks. It is one thing to be healed and another to be made whole. Settling for just healing is limiting your supply but wholeness through thanksgiving connects you to God's unlimited supply of whatever you need and will ever need. Wholeness should be your goal and your inheritance as a son or daughter of the King.

Gratitude brings Promotion

Whenever gratitude is expressed it reveals humility. It could be manifest in laying prostrate in worship, on your knees in prayer, bowing in acknowledgement, saying "thank you", or recognizing people who have helped you. Such humility makes God continue to lift you up. God resists the proud but gives grace to the humble and, if one humbles himself before Him, God will always lift him up.

Jesus humbled Himself, was always grateful to the Father, and was promoted. Therefore, "For this reason also, God highly exalted Him and bestowed on Him the name which is above every name, so that at the name of Jesus every knee will bow, of those who are in heaven and on earth and under the earth, and that every tongue will confess that Jesus Christ is Lord, to the glory of God the Father" (Phi 2: 9-11).

The ultimate strategy is to adopt the Jesus model.

GRATITUDE WHEN YOU FACE NEW CHALLENGES

When facing new challenges, gratitude becomes the stepping-stone for faith and courage, and a catalyst for victory. Gratitude takes our eyes off the problem and sets our sights on God. Our thanksgiving, gratitude, and prayer brings God into the equation. Fears, complaints, murmuring and negativity takes flight when we praise God because He inhabits the praises of His people.

So, as you praise, acknowledge, and boast of Him, He will come into the situation and reveal Himself as strong and mighty. As you thank and praise Him, faith and expectation are released for Him to demonstrate His power.

GRATITUDE IN PRAYER & WORSHIP

When we pray, we must always begin and end with gratitude. This simple practice produces mind-blowing results. Alice Walker said:

> *"Thank you is the best prayer that anyone could say. I say that one a lot. Thank you expresses extreme gratitude, humility and understanding."*

When we don't know what to say, let us just say, "thank you". We can't ask God for anything when we have not said, "thank you", for what He has already done. We enter and depart His gates with thanksgiving. "Be careful for nothing; but in everything, by prayer and supplication with thanksgiving, let your requests be made known unto God" (Phi 4:6). Without gratitude and thanksgiving, one's prayers are incomplete.

This practice and culture will guarantee results in prayer.

Gratitude while Facing the Impossible

Gratitude has the capacity of making the impossible possible. It releases resurrection power like at Lazarus' tomb. Jesus said, "Father I thank you that you hear me" (Joh 11:42), before commanding Lazarus to come forth. Hence, it was the power of thanksgiving that made the miracle possible.

The Syrophoenician woman worshipped and thanked Jesus for the crumbs and even though it wasn't time she was rewarded with an unscheduled miracle and breakthrough (Mark 7:25-30).

Jehoshaphat prayed and gave thanks to God saying, "Praise the Lord for His mercies endureth forever" and it released God's intervention (2 Chro 20:21).

Paul and Silas, even while in chains, they prayed and expressed gratitude to God and their praise activated the impossible to happen (Acts 16:25).

May the Lord do the impossible, miraculous, supernatural, divine, and the mind-blowing for you in this season and in many seasons to come. In Jesus' name, Amen!

> "Gratitude is a currency that we can mint for ourselves, and spend without fear of bankruptcy."
>
> **Fred De Witt Van Amburgh**

Conclusion

In the words of John F. Kennedy, one of the greatest leaders of the world, "as we express our gratitude, we must never forget that the highest appreciation is not to utter words but to live by them."

May God help us move from speech into action, individually and collectively bestowing gratitude to Him and humanity all the days of our lives for His name's sake and for His glory.

Thank you for reading this book and, more importantly, for practicing it every single day and teaching your children and the generations to come this Kingdom mystery and culture to guarantee victories and testimonies on earth and even in heaven.

Forever Grateful,
Archbishop Nicholas Duncan-Williams

www.ingramcontent.com/pod-product-compliance
Lightning Source LLC
Chambersburg PA
CBHW071520040426
42444CB00008B/1726